ALL ABOUT ME

My Family

JENNER

PROJECTS

W
FRANKLIN WATTS
LONDON · SYDNEY

First published in 2010
by Franklin Watts

Copyright © Franklin Watts 2010

Franklin Watts
338 Euston Road
London NW1 3BH

Franklin Watts Australia
Level 17/207 Kent Street
Sydney, NSW 2000

Series editor: Sarah Peutrill
Art director: Jonathan Hair
Design: www.rawshock.co.uk
Picture researcher: Kathy Lockley
Consultant: Molly Wolfe, Child Therapist

Dewey number: 306.8'7

ISBN: 978 0 7496 9518 7

Printed in China

Franklin Watts is a division of Hachette
Children's Books, an Hachette UK
company. www.hachette.co.uk

Credits: Abejon Photography/jabejon/iStockphoto:
6. Igor Balasanov/_IB_/iStockphoto: 15 Left.
Edouardo Jose Bernadino/azndc/iStockphoto: 17p
Bubbles Photolibrary/Alamy: 19 Bottom, 19 Top,
22. ClassicStock/Alamy: 14 Top. Corbis Yellow: 24.
digitalskillet/iStockphoto: 10. Diloute/iStockphoto:
11 Top. Jaimie Duplass/Shutterstock: 8. Xavier
Gallego/xavigm/iStockphoto: 7 Bottom Centre,
17r. geotrac/iStockphoto: 7 BottomLeft, 17n.
Golden Pixels LLC/Alamy: 9. Hachette Children's
Books: 21. Justin Horrocks/iStockphoto: 17m,
17q, 17s. imagematrix/iStockphoto: 17f. iofoto/
iStockphoto: 17a. Linda Kloosterhof/Linda
Yolanda/iStockphoto: 12. Elena Korenbaum/elkor/
iStockphoto: 17c. Kzenon/iStockphoto: Cover. Rich
Legg/LeggNet/iStockphoto: 17b. Dawn Liljenquist/
pink_cotton_candy/iStockphoto: 7 BottomRight,
17o. Steve Luker/iStockphoto: 7 Top Centre Right,
17k. Rob Marmion/Shutterstock: 14 Bottom.
Monkey Business Images/Shutterstock: 26. Aldo
Murillo/iStockphoto: 27 Bottom. naphtalina/
iStockphoto: 7 Top Right, 17l. Nossa Productions/
Corbis: 20 . parema/iStockphoto: 17h. Glenda
Powers/McIninich/iStockphoto: 18. Daniel
Rodriguez/theboone/iStockphoto: title page,
13. Gary Roebuck/Alamy: 25. Iain Sarjeant/
Northlightimages/iStockphoto: 15 Right
Steve Snowden/StevieS/iStockphoto: 17 Top.
Julie Vader/JEVader/iStockphoto: 17e. Jacob
Wackerhausen/iStockphoto: 7 Top Left, 17i.
Duncan Walker/duncan1890/iStockphoto: 7 Top
Centre Left, 17j. Franklin Watts/Chris Fairclough:
27 Top. Franklin Watts/Ray Moller: 11 Bottom.
Janine Wiedel Photolibrary/Alamy: 16. Brad
Wieland/iStockphoto: 17d. Rachel Willis/
DelphiM/iStockphoto: 17g. Catherine Yeulet/
monkeybusinessimages/iStockphoto: 23.

CONTENTS

(Words in **bold** are in the glossary on page 28.)

We are all part of a family. Our families are the people we live with. Every family is different and special.

This family has a mum and two children. Who is in your family?

THE PEOPLE IN A FAMILY

Families are made up of lots of different people - mums, dads, sisters, brothers, grannies, grandpas, and more. Some families have lots of people and some have a few. The people that you live with are your **immediate family**.

FAMILY TREE

You probably also have lots of family members - or **relatives** - who don't live with you, such as your grandparents or cousins. They are your **extended family**. They are all part of your family tree - and the tree gets bigger and bigger as it branches out to include more relatives.

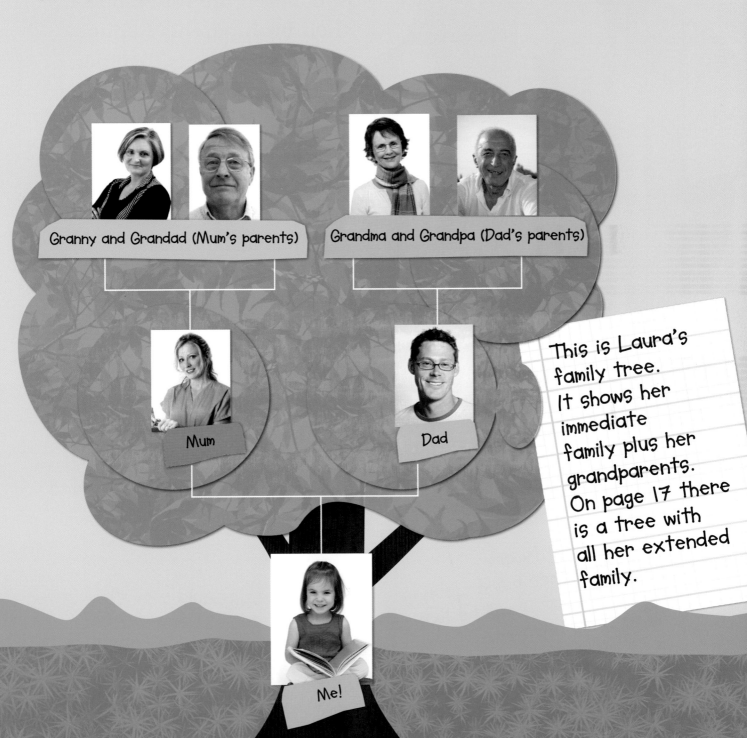

Granny and Grandad (Mum's parents)

Grandma and Grandpa (Dad's parents)

Mum

Dad

Me!

This is Laura's family tree. It shows her immediate family plus her grandparents. On page 17 there is a tree with all her extended family.

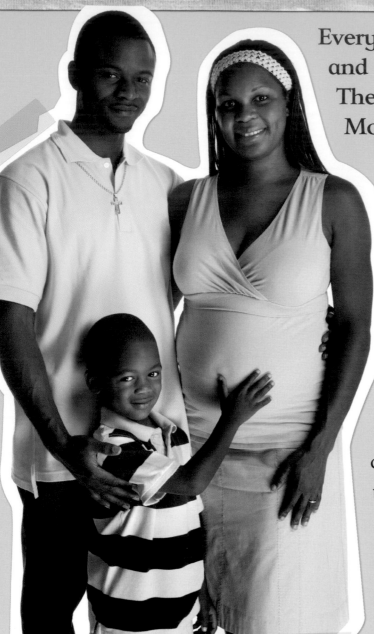

Everyone has to have a mum and dad in order to be born. They are your birth parents. Most children are raised by their birth parents - either by both parents together, or by one parent. Some children become part of another family.

MAKING BABIES

A man and a woman make a new baby when they come together in a special kind of cuddle. At first the baby is just a tiny speck. Then it grows inside the mum's tummy for about nine months - until at last the baby is born. Most parents have a baby because they love each other and they want to love a child as well.

Leon's parents are having another baby. Leon wonders what it will be like to be a big brother.

How would you feel if you were about to have a new baby in your family?

Helen and Philip adopted their daughter, Lily. They give her lots of love and Lily is very happy with her mum and dad.

ADOPTING CHILDREN

Sometimes a child's birth parents can't take care of him or her. The child may then be **adopted** by parents who can care for the child in a safe and loving home. The adoptive parents become the child's immediate family.

Some families include children adopted into the family and children born into the family.

All children need an adult to look after them, to give them a place to live, to keep them safe and healthy, and to make sure they eat and sleep and go to school. Parents are usually in charge of doing these things, but sometimes they need help.

Zack's dad helps him with his homework. He shows Zack how to work out the answers for himself.

A PARENT'S JOB

Parents act as a guide through childhood, helping their children to learn right from wrong. They try to teach and **encourage** their children - but also **discipline** them when necessary. Most parents agree that being a mum or dad is the best job in the world, but also the hardest.

Ruby's grandma takes care of her after school. They have lots of fun.

HELP WITH CHILDCARE

Your parents may need help looking after you. If grandparents live nearby, they might help with childcare. Some families have a childminder or nanny to look after the children while the parents are at work, and other children go to a club before and after school.

Who helps to look after you?

Kiera's childminder, Rachel, usually takes her to the park after school.

Many children also have brothers and sisters in their family. Brothers and sisters are also known as siblings. They may be older or younger than you, or the same age if you are a twin. Siblings are usually part of your immediate family.

A SPECIAL RELATIONSHIP

Brothers and sisters share a special **relationship**. Your siblings are a part of your life when you are children and when you grow up. Siblings help each other, have fun together and share lots of things that are special to your family.

Harry has two big sisters and a big brother. He loves having sisters and brothers around to play with!

SIBLING ARGUMENTS

Your relationship with your siblings can be like a seesaw, sometimes up and sometimes down. Siblings not only have to share toys and things, they also share their parents. Sometimes this means you fight to get attention from your parents. At other times, a brother or sister can be your best friend, someone who stands by you no matter what.

Sometimes, Mustapha fights with his little brother, Hamza. But most of the time, they just have fun fooling around.

 Do you have brothers or sisters? How do you get on with them?

You might call them Grandma and Grandpa, Gran and Grandad, Nanna and Poppa, or something else. They are your grandparents - your mum and dad's parents. You might even have great-grandparents - the parents of your grandparents!

Asha's mum says that her parents were very strict when she was growing up. Asha can't imagine her grandparents being strict!

An old picture shows Asha's mum when she was young, with Asha's gran, grandad and aunt.

This new picture shows Asha's mum now, with Asha, her grandad and her aunt.

OLDEN DAYS

Imagine your grandparents bringing up your mum and dad - reminding them to tidy their room or brush their teeth - just as your mum and dad are raising you now.

What do you think has changed since your parents were young, and what has stayed the same?

FUN WITH GRANDCHILDREN

Your grandparents may live nearby or far away. Sadly, some grandparents may be ill or have died. But many grandparents still enjoy time with their grandchildren. Grandparents often feel that they have already done the hard job of raising children (your parents) so now they can relax and spoil their grandchildren (you).

Although Lola's gran lives far away, Lola likes to phone her for a chat.

How many relatives have you got? Your extended family could go on and on. Some relatives may live nearby, some far away. Other relatives you probably haven't met.

Every year, lots of relatives come to Tamara's family get-together.

WHO'S WHO

- Aunts and uncles - your parents' sisters and brothers, and their **partners**
- Cousins - the children of your aunts and uncles
- Great-aunts and great-uncles - your parents' aunts and uncles
- Great-grandparents - your grandparents' mum and dad.

Sometimes we think of close adult friends as part of the family too, and we may call them 'Aunt' or 'Uncle'.

DIFFERENT GENERATIONS

You, your siblings and cousins, all belong to the youngest **generation**. As you go back in time, there is your parents' generation with your aunts and uncles, and then your grandparents' generation, and further back still to your great-grandparents' generation. Relatives from the past are called **ancestors**.

Great-grandparents (Mum's grandparents)

Great-grandparents (Dad's grandparents)

Granny and Grandad (Mum's parents)

Grandma and Grandpa (Dad's parents)

Aunt (Mum's sister)

Mum

Dad

Uncle and Aunt (Dad's brother and his wife)

You can see how it all adds up to a big family tree! How does this family tree compare to the family tree on page 7?

Me!

Cousins (Uncle and Aunt's children)

Families don't always stay the same. People change over time, and this means that families change too. They may gain new members and lose others.

ADDING FAMILY

When children are born or adopted, or when adults meet a new partner, these new members join the family. The family has to get used to the change. Babies, for example, may be small in size, but they make a big difference to the everyday life of a family, and to the relationships within the family.

Until his baby sister was born, Ali was the youngest in his family.

LOSING FAMILY

As time passes, people get older and die. If someone in your family dies, you will probably feel sad for a long time. After a while, the sadness will fade but your special memories will remain.

Zoe's grandfather died recently. She misses Gramps and his silly jokes.

WHEN PARENTS SEPARATE

Sometimes parents may decide that they no longer love each other, although they both love the children. When parents separate or **divorce** it affects the children too. It takes time to get used to the new life.

Wendy cried when her dad moved away. She's still getting used to not having him about.

Families are made up in lots of different ways. Members of the same family may live together or they may live apart.

TWO HOMES

If parents separate, one parent usually stays with the children, while the other moves out. Some children live part of the time with each parent, so they have two homes. Even though the parents might live apart, they still have to work together to make sure the children are well looked after.

? What kinds of things might children have to get used to if one parent moves away?

Dylan's parents are divorced. He lives with his mum most of the time...

... but he sees his dad at the weekends and in the school holidays.

STEP-FAMILIES

Some children are part of a **step-family**. If parents have separated, they may marry someone else. The new husband or wife becomes a step-father or step-mother to the children that are already in the family. If the step-parents also have children, they become step-sisters and step-brothers.

Sometimes, children may need to live apart from their family. They may live with a **foster family** until they can return to their birth family, or until they are adopted.

Nico's mum is married to Grace's dad, making Nico and Grace step-brother and step-sister. Last year, Nico's mum and Grace's dad had a baby together.
The baby is Nico and Grace's **half-sister**.

LIVING IN A FAMILY

Even when you love your family, it's sometimes hard to get along. It helps to think about other people, and be kind and considerate - it makes family life much more pleasant!

SHARING

Living together involves a lot of sharing - it can be sharing a bedroom, sharing toys, sharing the TV or even sharing chores. Simply put, it means sharing the family home. It helps to keep things tidy, help out around the house and not be greedy with your toys. If you are willing to share, it helps the family get along much better.

 **What do you like sharing with your family?**

Most of the time, Marta and Katrin like sharing and doing things together. They especially like sharing stories and giggles at bedtime.

During a family meal, Valerie and Chad take turns telling their parents about their day.

NOT ALL THE SAME

Just because you are related, doesn't mean that everyone in your family is all the same. You each have your own likes and dislikes. Although you may not agree with everyone in your family all of the time, it's important to listen to each other.

Keep a kindness chart for your family. Everyone – adult or child – can join in and add a star whenever they notice kind behaviour.

Special occasions are times for families to gather and celebrate. People often want to share their happiness with other members of the family.

Meredith and her relatives gave her grandmother and grandfather a surprise anniversary party!

CELEBRATING TOGETHER

Sometimes, the entire extended family gathers together. You may even have relatives living far away that you only see at special family celebrations.

What special times have you celebrated with your family?

WEDDINGS

When couples marry, they join together to become a family - and their extended families also join to make an even larger extended family. The bride and groom call each other's parents mother-in-law and father-in-law. A sibling by marriage is called a brother-in-law or sister-in-law.

Lots of family and friends celebrated Oscar and Isobel's wedding. They threw confetti to wish the couple good luck in their lives together as a brand—new family.

25

Being part of a family usually means that you've got people who care about you and a place to belong. Families should love and support each other - and have fun together.

HELPING EACH OTHER

Families should help each other and look after each other, in good times and bad. Make sure you tell them how much they mean to you. You may take it for granted that your family already know you love them, but it's always nice to hear!

If you can't ask your family for help try talking to another adult that you trust, such as a teacher or friend.

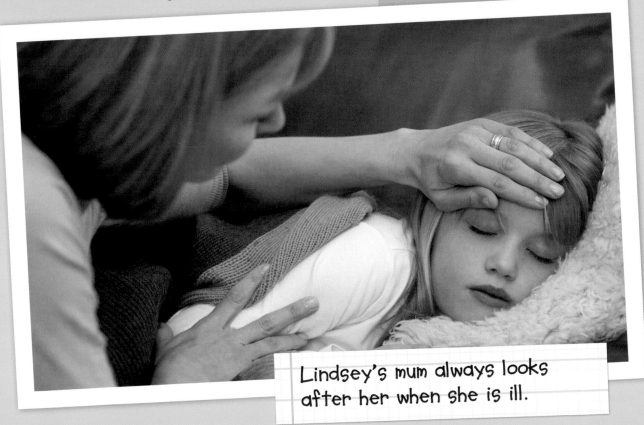

Lindsey's mum always looks after her when she is ill.

Seema likes playing board games with her big sister, Jamila.

TIME TOGETHER

Families are often very busy, but simply spending time together is important too. Having fun makes everyone feel good about themselves and about the other people in the family. Enjoying time together also leaves you with happy memories that you can all share in years to come.

Holly and her family go cycling together.

Ask if you can have a special family day to do something fun. What would you like to do?

Adopted becoming part of a family that is not the family you were born into.

Ancestors family relatives from the past.

Discipline teaching good behaviour.

Divorce when a husband and wife are not married any more.

Encourage to give someone hope and support by offering help and praise.

Extended family family members that are not as closely related to you, such as grandparents, aunts, uncles and cousins.

Foster family a family who looks after you but is not your own.

Generation a level of the family tree. For example, you, your brothers and sisters and cousins are the youngest generation.

Half-sister or half-brother siblings who share one birth parent.

Immediate family family members that you live with who are usually closely related to you, such as your mum, dad, sister or brother.

Partner a person that someone is married to or is having a relationship with.

Relationship how people get along with each other. For example, you have a different relationship with your mum than you do with your sisters and brothers.

Relatives people who are part of your family.

Siblings sisters and brothers.

Step-family a family in which a parent is married to a new partner. The new partner is the step-mother or step-father of the children, and the children are his or her step-children.

Websites

National Family Week -
bringing families together
www.nationalfamilyweek.co.uk

Family Links - transforming
schools and families
www.familylinks.org.uk

The Place 2 Be - school-based
counselling service, dedicated to
improving the emotional wellbeing
of children, their families and the
whole school community.
www.theplace2be.org.uk

Gingerbread - single parents,
equal families
www.gingerbread.org

Note to parents and teachers: Every effort has
been made by the Publishers to ensure that these
websites are suitable for children, that they are of the
highest educational value, and that they contain no
inappropriate or offensive material. However, because of
the nature of the Internet, it is impossible to guarantee
that the contents of these sites will not be altered. We
strongly advise that Internet access is supervised by a
responsible adult.

Books

'Meet the Family' series: *My Mum
My Dad, My Brother, My Sister
My Grandparents, My Aunt and
Uncle* by Mary Auld
(Franklin Watts)

What's My Family Tree? by Mick
Manning and Brita Granstrom
(Franklin Watts)

The Family Book by Todd Parr
(Little, Brown)

'How Can I Deal With' series: *My
Parents' Divorce, My Stepfamily,
Our New Baby, When People Die*
by Sally Hewitt (Franklin Watts)

*Why Should I Share?, Why Should
I Help?, Why Should I Listen?* by
Clare Llewellyn and Mike Gordon
(Wayland)

'My Family and Me' series:
*Celebrating A Birthday, Going
On Holiday, Sharing A Meal,
Welcoming A New Baby* by Mary
Auld (Franklin Watts)

INDEX